Flowchart Science

The RESPIRATORY SYSTEM

Richard and Louise Spilsbury

raintree
a Capstone company — publishers for children

Raintree is an imprint of Capstone Global Library Limited, a company incorporated in England and Wales having its registered office at 264 Banbury Road, Oxford, OX2 7DY – Registered company number: 6695582

www.raintree.co.uk
myorders@raintree.co.uk

Produced for Raintree by Calcium
Editors: Sarah Eason and Harriet McGregor
Designers: Paul Myerscough and Simon Borrough
Picture researcher: Rachel Bloun
Originated by Capstone Global Library Limited © 2018
Printed and bound in India

ISBN 978 1 4747 6584 8
22 21 20 19 18
10 9 8 7 6 5 4 3 2 1

British Library Cataloguing in Publication Data
A full catalogue record for this book is available from the British Library.

Acknowledgements
Cover art: Shutterstock: Denk Creative; Simon Borrough.
Picture credits: Shutterstock: Adriaticfoto 10, Subbotina Anna 24–25, Baciu 32b, Samuel Borges Photography 6, Borysevych.com 40bl, Hung Chung Chih 32–33, CKP1001 29, Cliparea/Custom Media 20, Luciano Cosmo 16, Decade3d - anatomy online 18–19, Designua 22, Extreme Sports Photo 11, Mandy Godbehear 26–27, Anna Grigorjeva 14–15, Antonio Guillem 44bl, India Picture 35c, Eric Isselee 34, Puwadol Jaturawutthichai 38b, Sebastian Kaulitzki 4–5, Gregory Kendall 27br, Kzenon 15tr, Lucky Business 40–41, Mavo 1, 28, Mimagephotography 38–39, NoPainNoGain 12–13, Chotwit piyapramote 36–37, SpeedKingz 12bl, Stockyimages 44–45, Max Topchii 4, Undrey 43, VectorsMarket 30, Adam Vilimek 18b, Vlue 21, Wire_man 25tr, Mahathir Mohd Yasin 7, Zizi_mentos 8.

Contents

Chapter 1

Looking at lungs

The human lungs are like an amazing machine. They can expand (grow bigger) to hold more than 6 litres (10 pints) of air. They take the **oxygen** from air that our bodies need to live and grow. Lungs give us life.

Humans need a constant supply of air. Without air a person would die within just a few minutes. The lungs work 24 hours a day to be sure we always have the oxygen we need. When an adult human is at rest, they breathe 12–20 times per minute. Humans, like most vertebrates (animals with backbones), have two lungs. The lungs are in the chest and they are protected by the bones that form the rib cage.

We can swim underwater for a short time, but we must come to the surface to breathe.

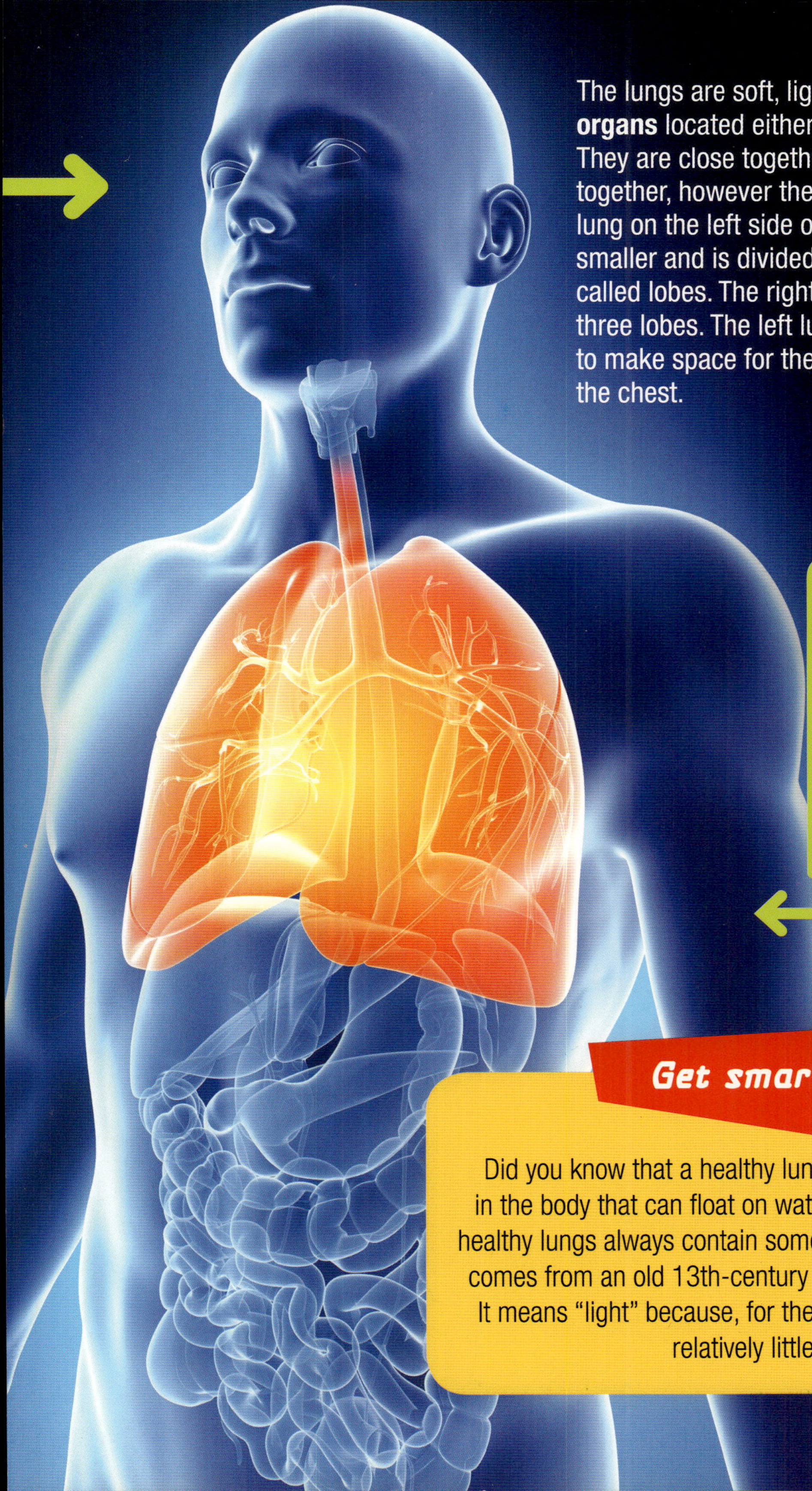

The lungs are soft, light, spongy and stretchy **organs** located either side of the heart. They are close together because they work together, however they are not identical. The lung on the left side of the body is slightly smaller and is divided into two sections called lobes. The right lung is divided into three lobes. The left lung is slightly smaller to make space for the heart, which is also in the chest.

Lungs vary in size, as people do, but adult lungs usually measure about 25–35 cm (10–14 inches) long and 10–15 cm (4–6 inches) wide.

Get smart!

Did you know that a healthy lung is the only organ in the body that can float on water? That is because healthy lungs always contain some air. The word "lung" comes from an old 13th-century European language. It means "light" because, for their size, lungs weigh relatively little.

Lungs for life

As soon as a baby is born, he or she takes their first big breath of air, filling their lungs with air for the very first time in their life. From birth onwards, people breathe in and out every few seconds every day for their entire life.

The human body needs to breathe in air because it requires a supply of oxygen to be able to get **energy** from food.

A baby's first breath is very important. During pregnancy, a baby's lungs are filled with fluid. When they are born they must suddenly fill with air.

Lungs remove oxygen from the air. The oxygen passes into the blood and circulates around the body. The blood distributes it to the body's **cells**, the tiny building blocks from which all body parts are made. The oxygen is combined with glucose, a type of sugar that the body gets from breaking down food in the process of digestion. When oxygen and glucose are combined, energy is released. The body needs energy for everything it does: to live, grow and work.

Using oxygen to release energy from food is called respiration. The parts of the body involved in this amazing process are known together as the respiratory system. During the process of respiration, wastes such as **carbon dioxide** are produced. The respiratory system is used to expel them into the air.

After we have eaten, the respiratory system helps us turn that food into fuel.

Get smart!

It is possible to survive with just one lung. Having one lung can limit your physical ability. People with one lung may not be able to do a lot of strenuous exercise. They should, however, be able to live a relatively normal life and live as long as someone with two lungs.

Get flow chart smart!

Breathing and respiration

The steps in this flow chart show how breathing and respiration work.

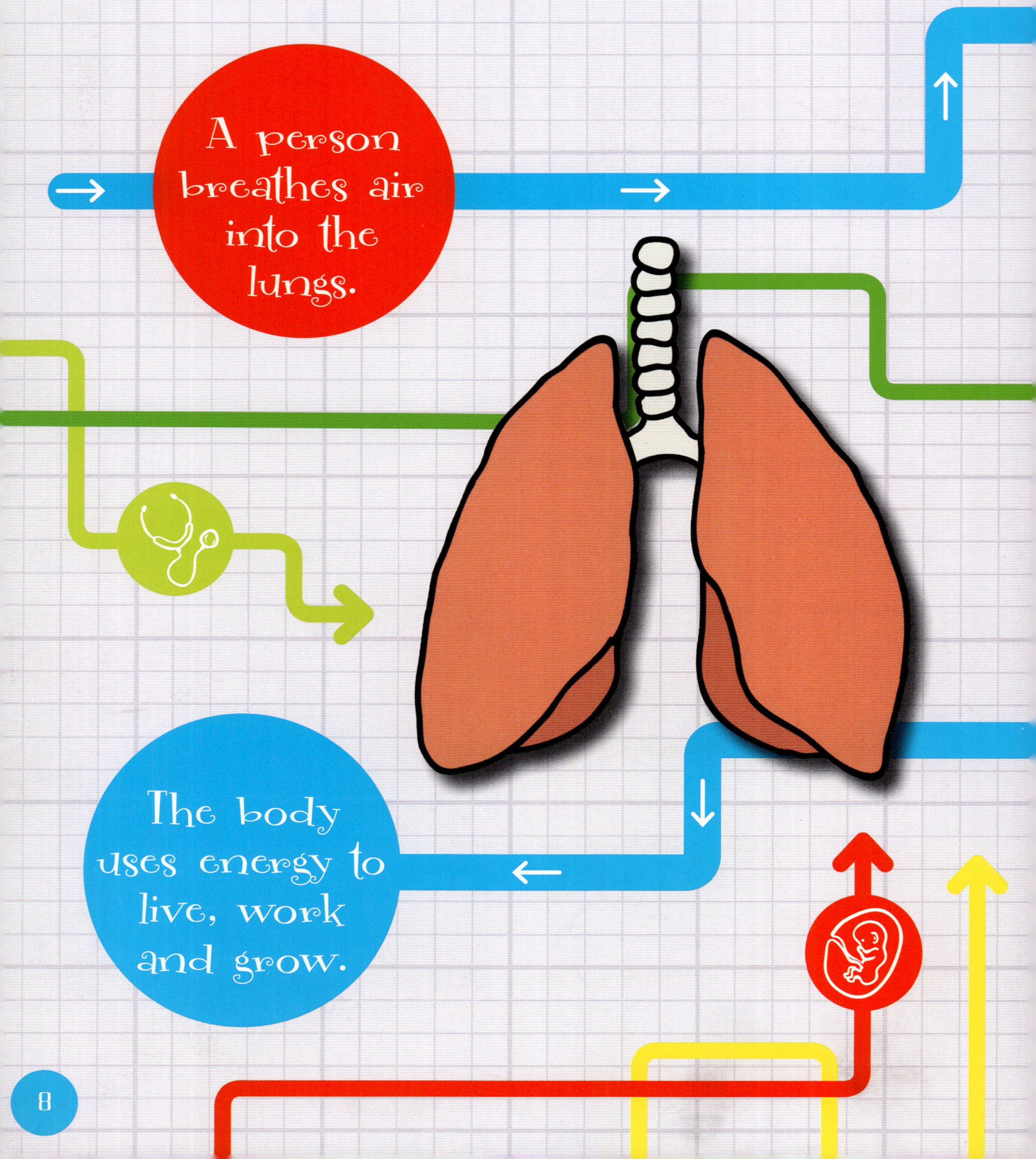

The lungs take oxygen from the air. The oxygen passes into the blood.

The blood distributes oxygen to the body's cells.

The cells combine oxygen with glucose to release energy.

Flowchart Smart

Chapter 2
Breathing

We inhale and exhale air around 22,000 times every day. The average person breathes in almost 11,000 litres (20,000 pints) of air every day. Breathing is an important part of the respiratory process and although it seems simple, it is very complex. It begins with the nose.

People mostly breathe in air through the nose, and into a space called the nasal cavity, behind the nose. As air passes through the nose, fine hairs and a sticky substance called mucus lining the nose **filter** it. The mucus traps dirt and dust to keep these particles from entering the lungs, where they could cause damage or disease. From the nasal cavity, air moves to the **trachea**, a tube that runs from the back of the throat down the chest to the lungs.

A sneeze can shoot air out at 161 km per hour (100 mph)!

Sometimes, if particles of dust, pepper or pollen irritate the inside of the nose, **nerve** endings inside the nose send a message to the brain. The brain tells the body to sneeze. Muscles in the chest push onto the lungs, so they send a blast of air up and out through the nose. When people sneeze, especially if they have a cold, the moist air that shoots out can contain dirt and germs. This is why it is best to catch a sneeze in a tissue and wash your hands afterwards.

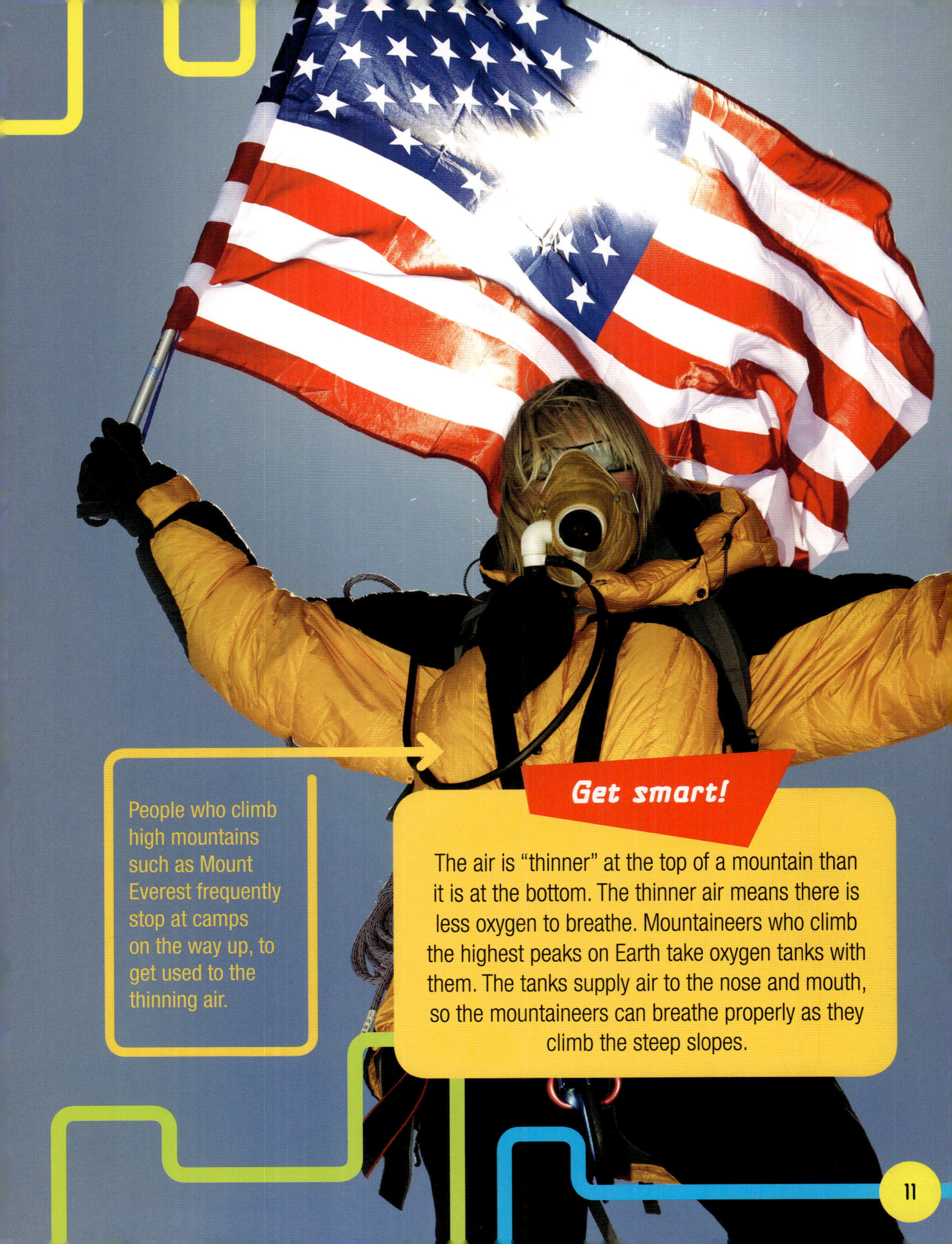

People who climb high mountains such as Mount Everest frequently stop at camps on the way up, to get used to the thinning air.

Get smart!

The air is "thinner" at the top of a mountain than it is at the bottom. The thinner air means there is less oxygen to breathe. Mountaineers who climb the highest peaks on Earth take oxygen tanks with them. The tanks supply air to the nose and mouth, so the mountaineers can breathe properly as they climb the steep slopes.

How breathing works

To take air into the body, muscles in the chest work a little like a pump. They suck air into the lungs and push it out again.

The **diaphragm** is a big band of dome-shaped muscle located between the stomach and the chest. To breathe in, the diaphragm contracts (squeezes) to become smaller. As it tightens it moves downwards towards the stomach, creating more space for the lungs. At the same time, rib muscles pull the ribs up and out, which also enlarges the space in the chest. This reduces the air **pressure** in the chest and lungs. Gases flow from areas of high pressure to areas of low pressure, so air flows in through the nose or mouth to the lungs.

The diaphragm contracts and moves down. The rib cage moves out. Air enters the lungs.

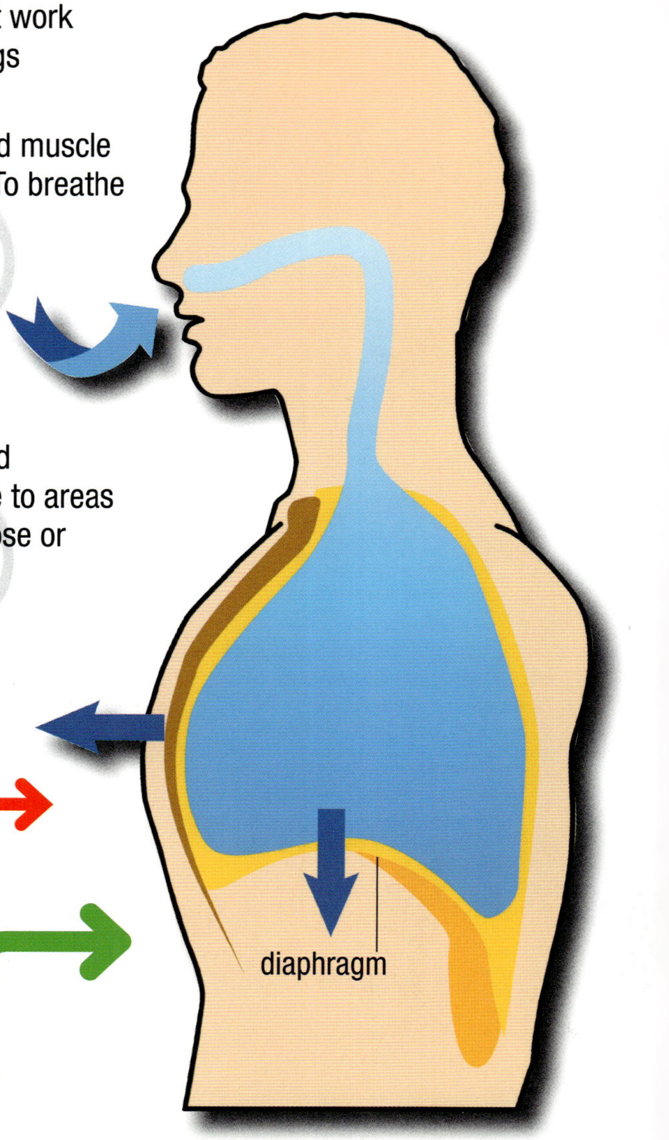

A foot pump expands when full of air. When it is pressed, the space inside is made smaller and air is forced out. Lungs also expand with air and then push out air by reducing in size.

To breathe out, the diaphragm relaxes and moves upwards and the rib muscles relax so that the rib cage lowers. This reduces the space in the chest.

When we breathe air into the lungs, it travels through two large tubes called **bronchi** at the bottom of the trachea. The inner walls of the bronchi are covered in small hairs called **cilia**. The cilia wave back and forth, spreading mucus into the throat and lungs. Mucus helps clean out the lungs and rid them of unwanted particles.

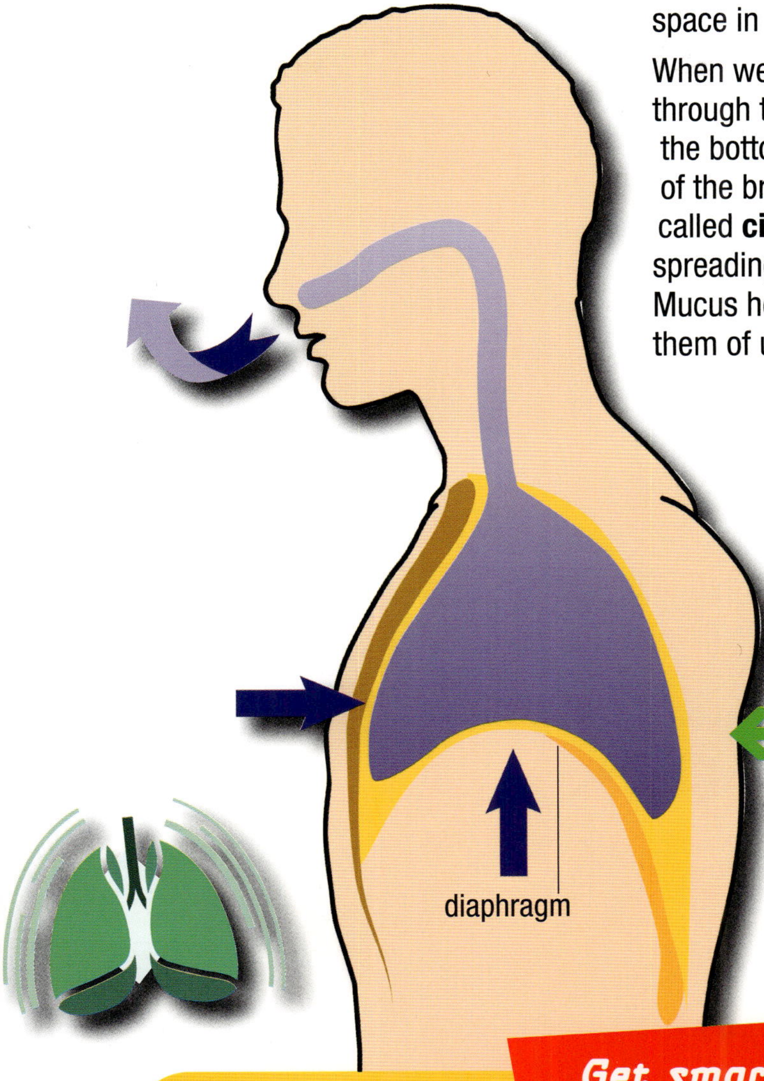

When the diaphragm and rib cage relax, the air pressure in the lungs increases. Air flows out from the lungs through the nose or mouth.

Get smart!

You get hiccups when something irritates the diaphragm, such as eating too quickly or too much. When this happens, the diaphragm contracts suddenly, making you breathe in air very quickly and suddenly. When the air that is speeding into your throat hits the glottis (the opening between your vocal cords), the glottis closes suddenly making the sound of the hiccup.

Fast and slow

Breathing is an involuntary action. This means that most of the time, we do not think about breathing in and out. It just happens. Sometimes, the brain changes our breathing rates without us thinking about it. It is also possible to control our breathing with our minds.

We are born with the ability to breathe even when we sleep. When asleep, the breathing rate (how many breaths we take per minute) slows down.

Get smart!

Try this breathing technique to help you relax. Breathe in slowly and gently, counting steadily from one to five. Then, let out your breath slowly, counting from one to five again. Each time, breathe in through your nose letting your breath flow deep down into your lungs. Breathe out through your mouth. Do this for 3–5 minutes.

Breathing is controlled by a respiratory control centre at the base of the brain. This control centre sends signals along nerves down the spinal cord to the muscles that work the diaphragm and rib cage. The signals ensure the muscles contract and relax regularly to make us breathe in (inhale) and breathe out (exhale) approximately once every 5 seconds.

Pedalling a bike causes the breathing rate to increase so more oxygen reaches the muscles.

Breathing rate can change with activity. The more active someone is, the more oxygen is needed by the active muscles. Sensors in the arm and leg muscles check how fast they are moving and send signals to the brain to cause the breathing rate to increase as necessary. Emotions can also change the breathing rate. Someone who is scared or angry will breathe faster. This gives them more energy in case they need it for a fight or to run away.

During periods of sleep, only a small amount of energy is necessary for body processes. This is why the breathing rate slows. Sometimes we choose to control our breathing. We might suck in air and then hold our breath so that we can stop breathing and swim underwater for a short time. Some people also practise breathing more slowly, gently and regularly to help them relax.

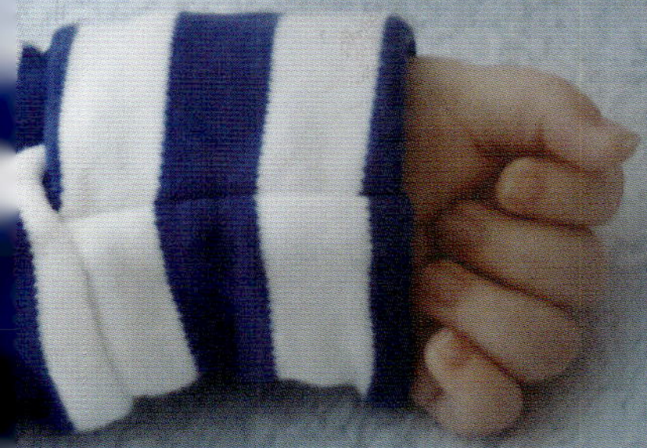

Get flow chart smart!

Inhale and exhale

Follow this flow chart to remind yourself how people breathe in and out.

To inhale, the diaphragm contracts, pulling down to increase the space in the chest.

At the same time, the muscles between the ribs contract, expanding the rib cage.

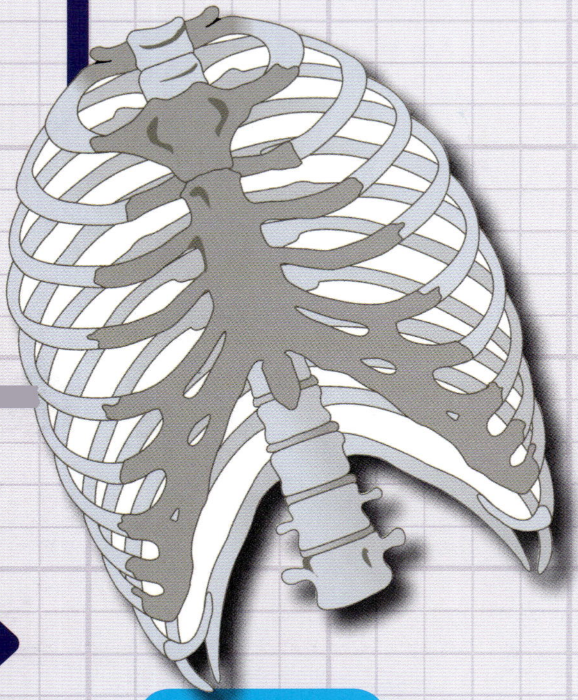

The pressure inside the chest increases and air is forced out.

The pressure inside the chest is lowered and air is sucked into the lungs.

To exhale, the diaphragm relaxes, moves upwards and reduces the space in the chest.

The muscles between the ribs relax and the rib cage drops inwards and down.

Flowchart Smart

Chapter 3

Oxygen delivery

Once air is inhaled, the lungs move oxygen into the blood. Then the blood delivers the oxygen around the body.

\Within the lungs, the bronchi branch off into smaller and smaller tubes. The smallest tubes are called **bronchioles**. There are about 30,000 bronchioles in each lung and many are thinner than a human hair. At the end of each of the bronchioles there are **alveoli**. Alveoli are tiny, spongy pouches. Each is so small that it can only be seen with the help of a powerful microscope. **Capillaries** surround the alveoli. Capillaries are the smallest type of **blood vessel** in the human body.

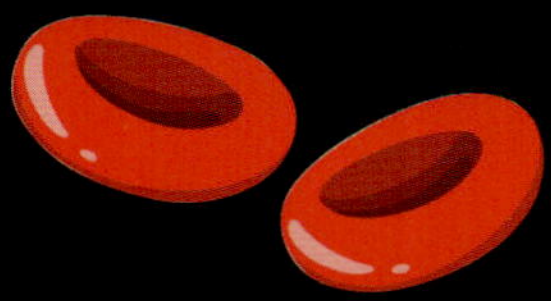

If the alveoli in a pair of lungs were stretched out flat, they would cover the entire area of a tennis court.

Get smart!

There are 600 million alveoli in an adult's two lungs. Scientists say that if all the capillaries surrounding the alveoli were unwound and placed end to end, they would cover an incredible 992 kilometres (616 miles).

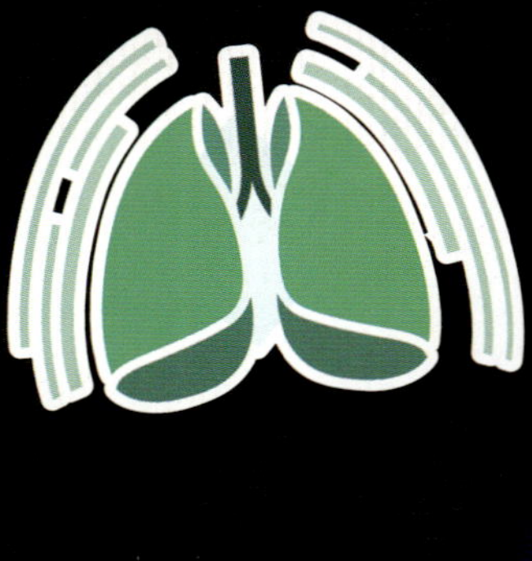

The walls of the alveoli and the capillaries are very, very thin. Oxygen passes through the walls of the alveoli and into the capillaries. This movement is called **diffusion**. It happens when there is more oxygen in the alveoli than in the capillary next to it. The oxygen passes into the capillary to try to balance out the difference. As we continue to breathe, we keep supplying the alveoli with more oxygen. The blood in the capillary is constantly flowing, carrying oxygen with it. This means that there is a continuous movement of oxygen from the alveoli into the capillaries.

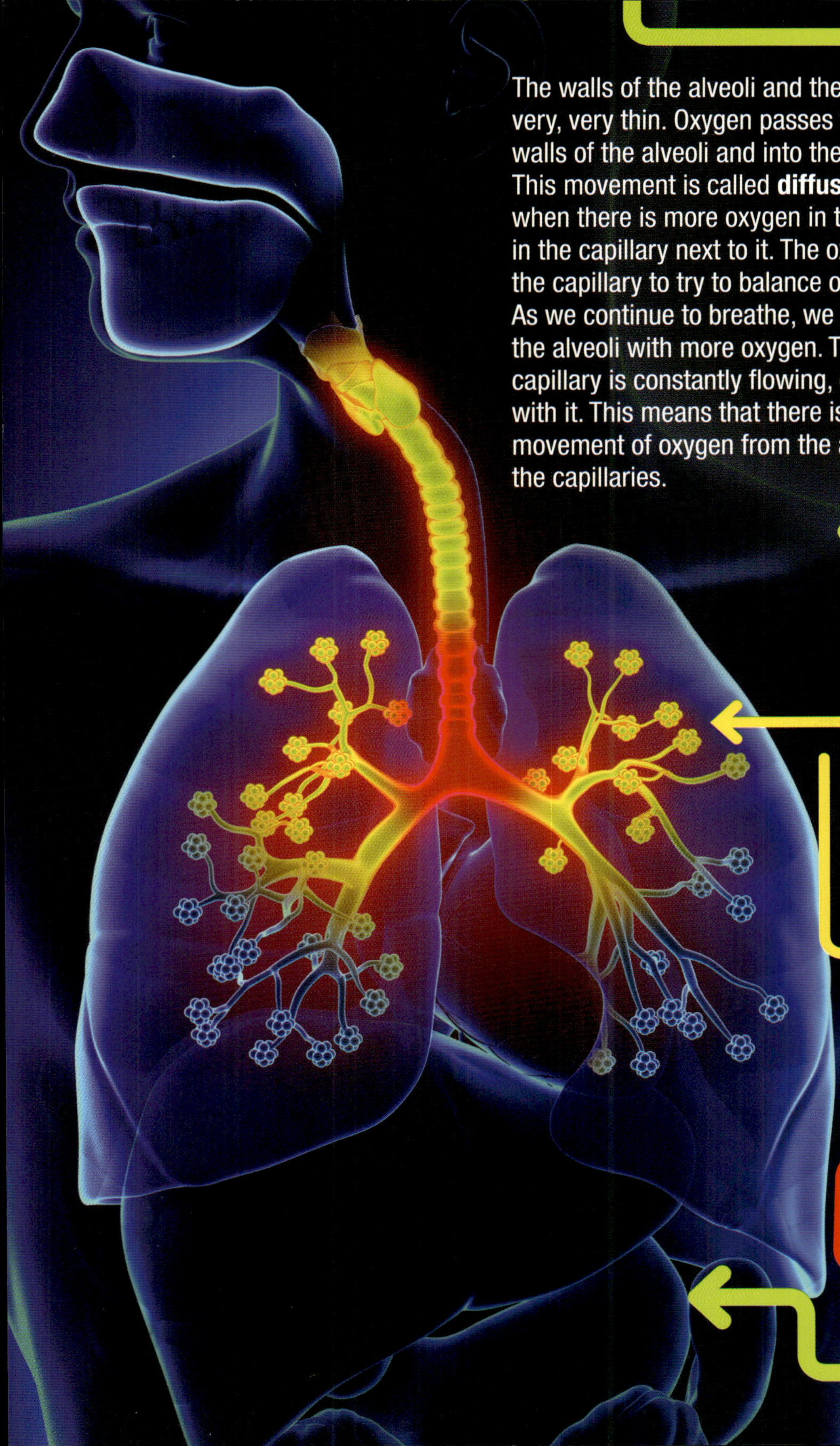

The trachea branches into two bronchi and many bronchioles and alveoli.

Blood transportation

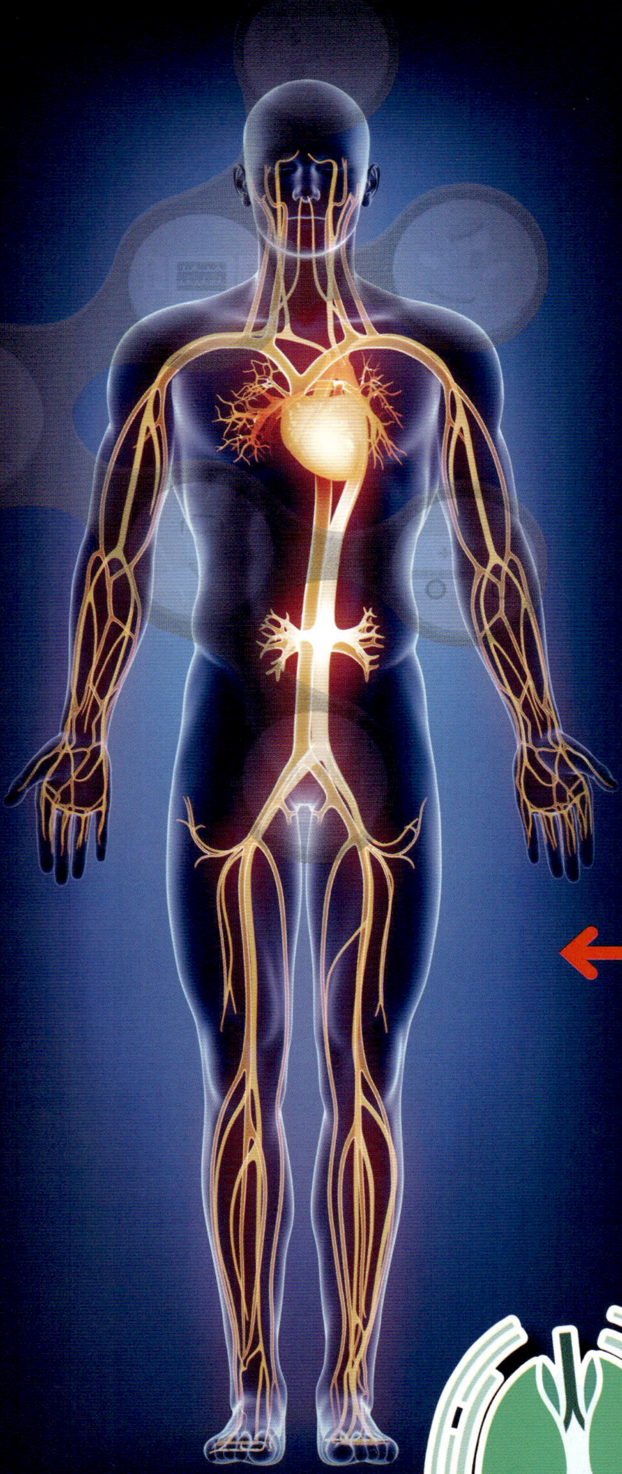

The blood is a little like the human body's delivery service. The heart pumps blood with enough force to make it flow all around the body, delivering oxygen to the body's cells.

The respiratory system and the **circulatory system** are closely connected. The respiratory system allows air to pass in and out of the body. It allows oxygen and carbon dioxide to be exchanged so cells can function. But, this would not happen without the help of the circulatory system, which consists of the heart and the network of blood vessels that carry oxygen around the body.

There are about 5 litres (10 pints) of blood in the human body. The blood travels continuously through blood vessels around the circulatory system.

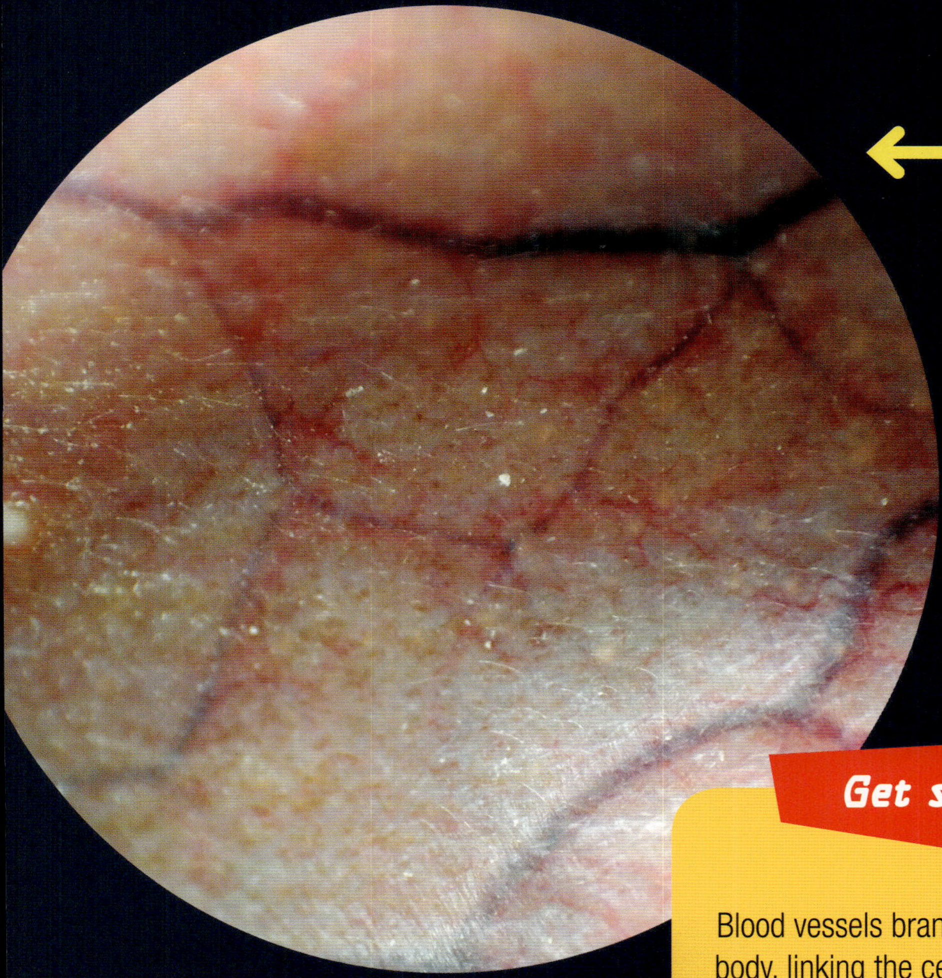

We can see some of the different sized blood vessels just beneath the surface of the skin.

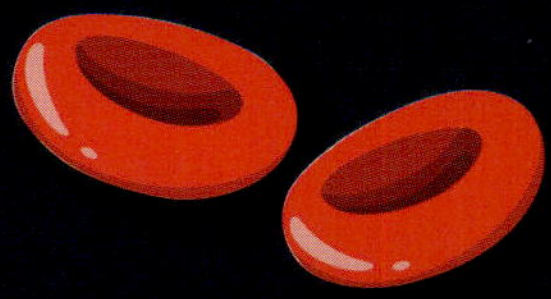

Get smart!

Blood vessels branch out all around the body, linking the cells of our organs and other body parts. If you laid out an adult's blood vessels in a line, that line would be almost 100,000 kilometres (60,000 miles) long. That is the equivalent of travelling 2.5 times around Earth. In adults, about 80,000 kilometres (50,000 miles) of those blood vessels are capillaries.

Blood pumped from the heart goes straight to the lungs, where it passes through the capillaries and collects oxygen. Oxygen is carried in red blood cells, one of the parts of blood. Red blood cells are red because they contain **haemoglobin**. The haemoglobin captures oxygen when blood passes through the lungs. Red blood cells are about the same size as the capillaries, so they move through capillaries in single-file.

Get flow chart smart!

Oxygen movement

This flow chart explains how blood carries oxygen from the lungs to the body's cells.

In the lungs, air passes down bronchioles into the alveoli.

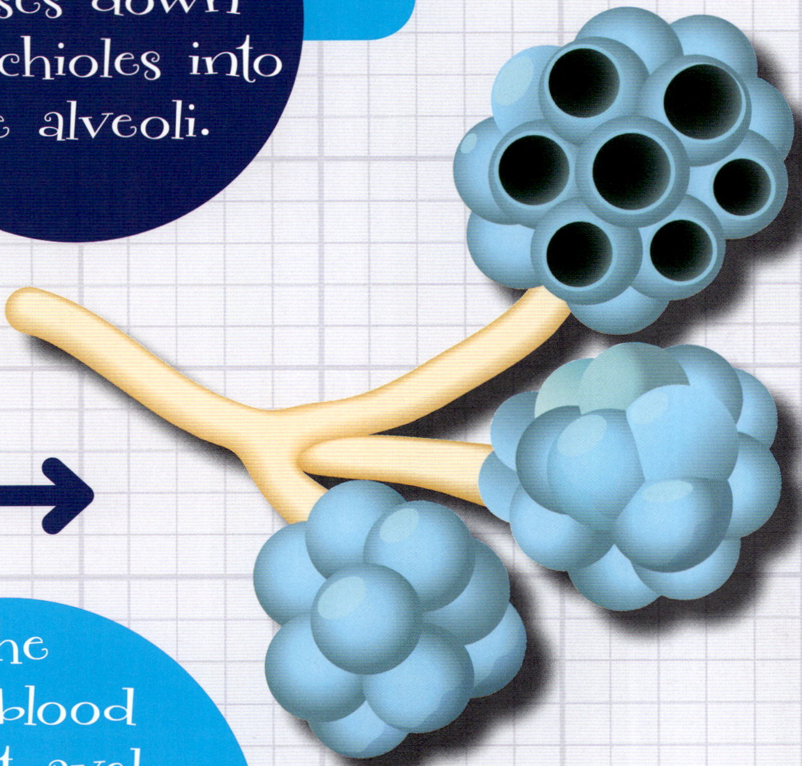

The red blood cells travel in the blood all around the body, delivering oxygen to the cells.

Oxygen moves through the walls of the alveoli and into the capillaries that surround them.

Haemoglobin in the red blood cells inside the capillaries captures the oxygen.

Flowchart Smart

Chapter 4

From fuel to energy

Blood delivers oxygen to the cells. The cells use it to obtain the energy they need to live and grow. The process of releasing energy from food is called respiration.

Energy is released from the food we eat inside the cells. The structures in a cell that carry out this process are **mitochondria**. Mitochondria are like the powerhouses of a cell. Inside the mitochondria a **chemical reaction** takes place between a type of sugar called glucose, which the body gets from the food we eat, and oxygen. This creates the energy necessary for the cell to carry out its functions.

Everyday activities would be impossible without energy. To get energy we need glucose and oxygen.

These mitochondria are found within cells. There are between 1,000 and 2,000 mitochondria in a typical cell.

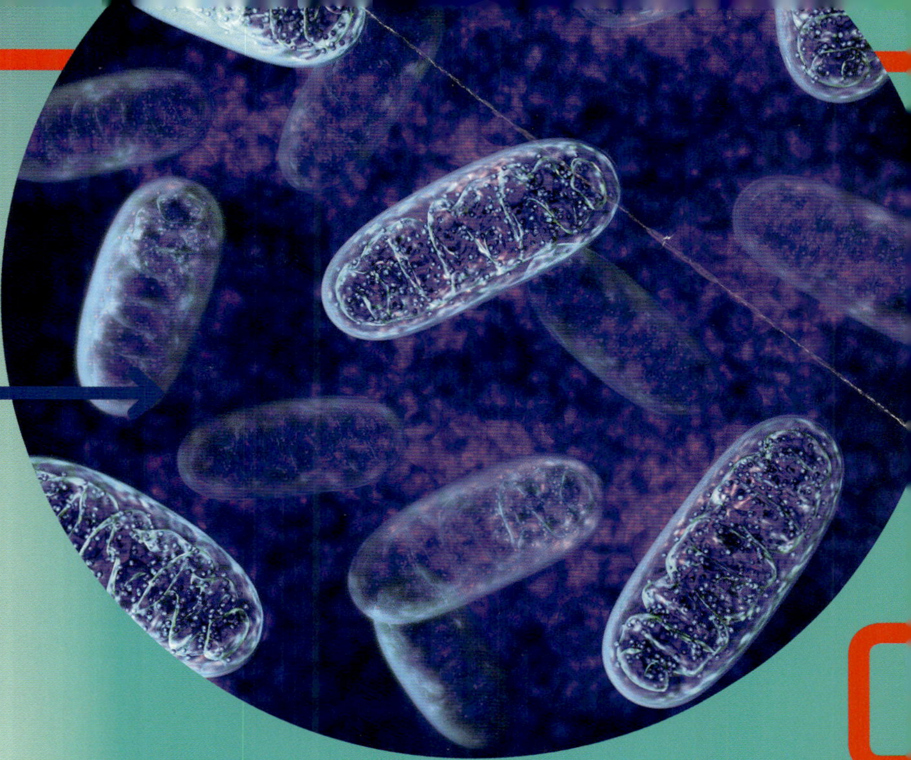

Mitochondria are dotted throughout cells. Some cells have more mitochondria than others. Some types of fat cells have many mitochondria because they store a lot of energy. Muscles also have many mitochondria because they need to release large amounts of energy to work, for example when we play sport or run a race.

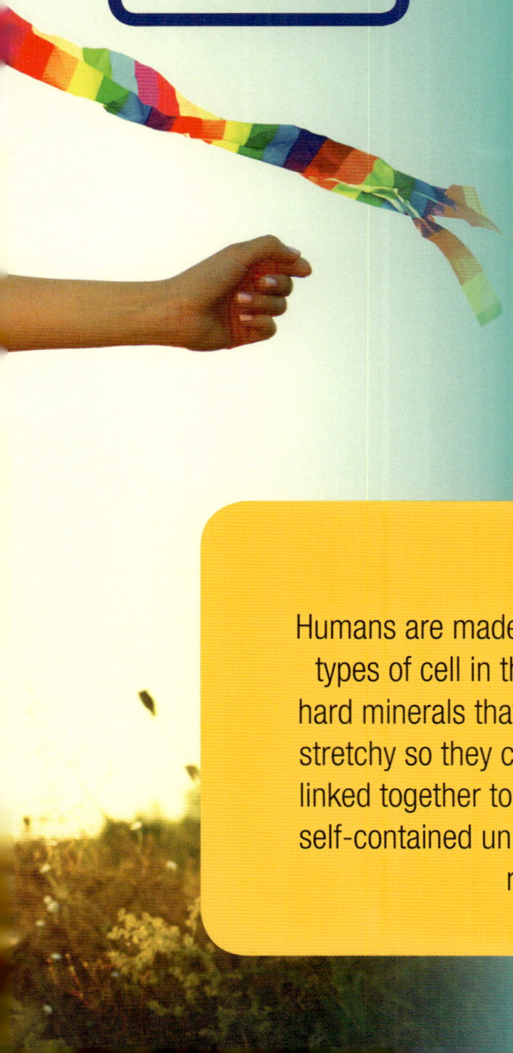

Get smart!

Humans are made up of about 100 trillion cells. There are many different types of cell in the human body. Bone cells are surrounded by rings of hard minerals that give bones their strength. Muscle cells are strong and stretchy so they can contract and relax. Nerve cells are long, narrow and linked together to carry signals to different parts of the body. All cells are self-contained units that can release energy from food so they can grow, repair and make copies of themselves.

Feel the heat

We use the energy released in cells during **respiration** for many processes, from powering the heart to keeping the brain working. Respiration also produces heat, which humans need to maintain a warm body temperature.

Humans are warm-blooded animals. The core (central part) of the body usually stays at a constant temperature of 37°C (98.6°F). This is the temperature at which the body functions efficiently. When someone is ill, they may have a **fever**. The body uses energy to create extra heat. This is part of the body's defence mechanism against **viruses** or **bacteria**. The high temperature helps destroy the germs.

In cold weather, your toes, nose and fingers may feel cold but your core temperature remains warm. Clothes help to keep the heat in.

Get smart!

Cold-blooded animals, such as lizards and snakes, use less energy because their bodies change temperature with their surroundings. They do not make their own body heat. Instead, they rely on sitting in the morning sun to warm up after a cold night.

Making energy releases heat. For example, when it is cold, the body shivers. Shivering happens when muscles contract and relax rapidly. Doing this increases the rate of respiration in muscle cells. This releases extra energy, which creates heat and warms the surrounding blood and tissues.

When the human body becomes too hot, the capillaries in the skin widen, and the amount of blood flowing through them increases. In this way, excess heat is released into the air to cool down the body.

People may look red during exercise. This is because the blood vessels near the surface of the skin have widened. The body's cells release extra heat during exercise and this is released to the air from the blood and skin.

Waste not, want not

When a fuel such as wood is burned in oxygen, it is not only heat energy that is produced. The process also releases waste in the form of smoke and fumes. Something similar happens when body cells use oxygen to release energy from food fuel. This process produces carbon dioxide and water as waste products.

When we breathe out on a cold day our breath looks misty because the waste water vapour condenses in cold air and turns back into droplets of liquid water.

People lose almost 0.5 litres (1 pint) of water a day through breathing.

The waste products of respiration diffuse out of the cells and into the blood. A substance in the blood called plasma collects the waste products. This liquid makes up about 55 per cent of the blood.

In the bloodstream, the plasma and waste travel to the heart. The heart pumps the blood to the lungs. Inside the lungs, carbon dioxide and water diffuse out of the blood and into the **alveoli**. The waste products pass up through the bronchioles, bronchi, trachea and throat and are breathed out through the nose and mouth.

Get smart!

When blood collects oxygen from the lungs and is first pumped around the body by the heart, it is rich in oxygen and bright-red in colour. The blood that flows back to the heart, after losing oxygen to the cells, contains far less oxygen. It also contains waste products, so it is no longer bright red, but more of a rusty colour.

Get flow chart smart!

Respiration

Follow the steps in this flow chart to see how respiration works.

When oxygen passes into the mitochondria inside the body's cells, a chemical reaction takes place between glucose and oxygen. This process releases energy for the cells to function.

Respiration produces heat, which we need to maintain our warm body temperature.

The waste products are breathed out through the nose and mouth.

When the cells in the body respire (use oxygen to release energy from food), carbon dioxide and water are produced as waste products.

Waste products diffuse from the cells into plasma in the blood.

Blood carrying the waste travels to the heart and lungs. At the lungs, carbon dioxide and water diffuse out of the blood and into the alveoli.

Flowchart Smart

Chapter 5

Breathing

The lungs are strong, hard-working organs that never rest, but they can be damaged if they are attacked by substances from outside the body, such as dirt and germs.

Air pollution is any harmful substance in the air, such as carbon dioxide fumes from car exhausts or factory chimneys. Air pollution can irritate, inflame or damage lungs. People who have lung disease, babies and the elderly are most at risk from air pollution. Even low levels of air pollution can cause health problems if someone is exposed to them for a long time. Air pollution can cause coughing and a feeling of breathlessness.

Get smart!

Farmer's lung is a condition caused by dust from mouldy hay, straw and grain. At first, it can feel like a simple cold, but if left untreated it can cause permanent lung damage. It happens when the lungs become hypersensitive to substances breathed in, and become inflamed. People who keep birds can get "bird fancier's lung", which is caused by breathing in particles from feathers or bird droppings. This causes inflammation to the **alveoli**.

When hay is left in bad weather, and then harvested, it may contain mould spores that cause farmer's lung.

Bronchitis and pneumonia are lung diseases. Bronchitis occurs when the bronchi become infected, irritated and inflamed. The walls of the bronchi produce mucus to trap dust and other particles that could otherwise get into the lungs. An **infection** makes them produce more mucus, which the body tries to remove by coughing. Pneumonia is the swelling of the tissue in one or both lungs. It is usually caused by a bacterial infection. The alveoli become **inflamed** and filled with fluid. Pneumonia is dangerous because it makes it harder for the lungs to absorb oxygen from air.

When cars are left running in traffic, they release exhaust fumes into the air, which can be damaging to pedestrians.

Asthma

Air usually moves in and out of lungs easily because the tubes inside the body that carry the air are round, open and clear. Asthma is a common condition that affects the lungs. In an asthmatic person, the tubes become narrower, making it hard for that person to breathe.

There are usually specific triggers that bring on an asthma attack. These include house-dust mites, animal fur, pollens, cigarette smoke, strong smells, gases, cold air, exercise and chest infections. An asthmatic person has extra-sensitive breathing tubes. When exposed to their particular trigger, the tubes temporarily become narrow and clogged with sticky mucus.

Cats are a common trigger for asthma. Asthma sufferers react to the flakes of skin known as dander in an animal's fur.

During an asthma attack, the narrowed airways make it hard to breathe in air. The person may wheeze (make a whistling sound when breathing), be breathless and cough a lot. They may feel like a band is tightening around their chest. After an asthma attack, the airways usually return to normal within a few days. One way for us to prevent asthma attacks is to avoid the triggers, but this is not always possible.

To use an inhaler, the patient puts the device into his or her mouth. They press the trigger on the top and breathe in at the same time. The medicine is breathed in.

Get smart!

Asthma can be controlled using medicines. The most common asthma treatments are taken using an inhaler. This is a small device that delivers a spray or powder medicine directly to the breathing tubes. There are two types of medicine: one to reduce the chance of an asthma attack and another to provide relief during an attack.

Get flow chart smart!

Asthma attack

This flow chart follows the steps that happen when someone has an asthma attack.

A person with asthma goes to a friend's house where there is a cat.

It becomes harder to breathe so the person coughs, wheezes and starts to feel their chest tighten.

They breathe in medicine from an inhaler. It opens the airways and helps them breathe more easily again.

They breathe in **allergens** from the cat fur that irritate their sensitive airways.

The breathing tubes swell and narrow and begin to produce sticky mucus.

Flowchart Smart

Chapter 6

Taking care of lungs

Lungs do an amazing job. If you take good care of your lungs, they can stay healthy throughout your whole life.

Lungs protect themselves with sticky mucus that lines the airways. It traps dust and germs and stops them entering the lungs. Cilia brush the mucus away from the lungs and towards the throat. Breathing in a lot of smoke, dust, fumes or chemicals, however, can cause problems. These substances damage the lungs and can cause scarring. These scarred areas no longer work properly. To keep lungs healthy, try to avoid areas with very high levels of pollution.

This x-ray shows the lungs. The dark areas are healthy. The white area on the right is not healthy. This patient has lung cancer.

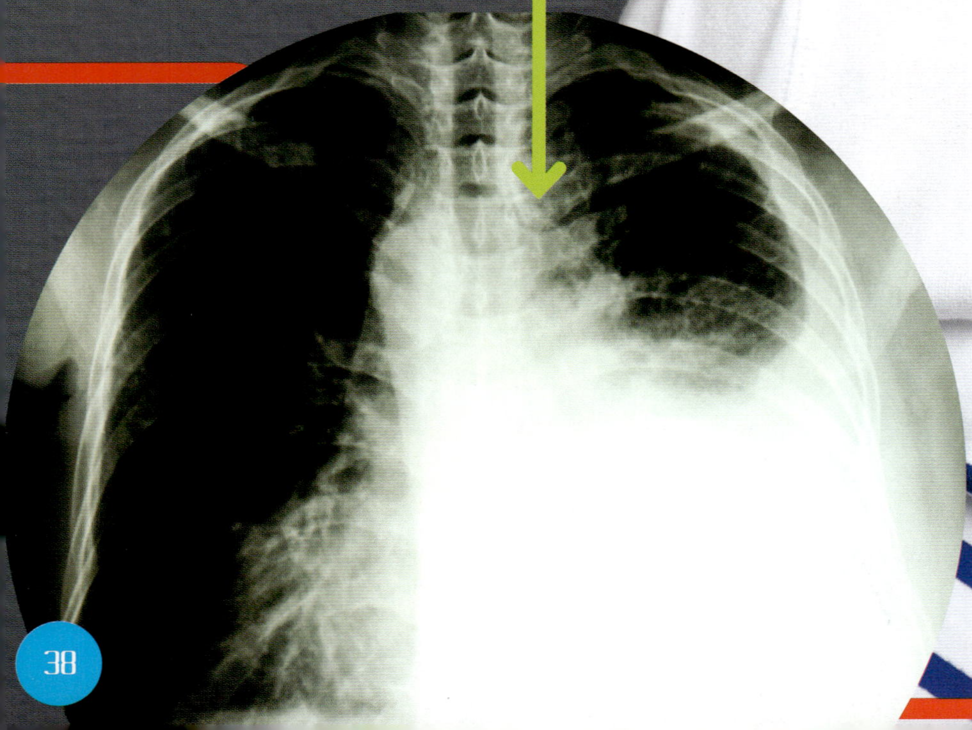

Keeping your lungs healthy can be fun. Laughter is great exercise for your lungs.

Smoking cigarettes is extremely damaging to the lungs. Cigarette smoke can break down the walls of the alveoli. This makes it harder for the body to take oxygen into the blood. Cigarette smoke also damages the cells of the lungs and may trigger changes that grow into lung cancer, a condition that can be fatal. Cigarette smoking is the biggest cause of lung cancer. Each year, about 1.4 million people are diagnosed with lung cancer, although not all of them as a result of smoking.

Get smart!

Did you know that plants can help clean the air and fill it with oxygen? Plants make their own food in a process called photosynthesis. They take carbon dioxide from the air and combine it with water that they collect through their roots. The waste product of photosynthesis is oxygen. So, not only do plants remove carbon dioxide from the air, but they also add more oxygen!

Energy for exercise

Lung capacity is the total amount of air that the lungs contain after a big breath in. People with a large lung capacity can send oxygen around their body faster. You can increase your lung capacity with regular exercise.

Aerobic means "relating to oxygen". Aerobic exercise makes people breathe harder and increase their heart rate in order to pump more oxygen around the body in the blood. Aerobic exercise includes running, football, basketball, swimming and dancing. These sports make you feel breathless because they cause your lungs to work hard. If you can, do some aerobic exercise at least three times each week to help improve your lung capacity.

At rest, you breathe around 15 times a minute. During exercise, you breathe 40–60 times a minute.

Learning to play a wind instrument, such as a clarinet, gives your lungs a great workout.

Get smart!

Another way to give your lungs a regular workout and help increase your lung capacity is to learn to play a wind instrument. A wind instrument is one that is played by blowing. When people play wind instruments, such as clarinets, saxophones, flutes or mouth organs, they must use their lungs' capacity to the fullest. This works the diaphragm and keeps the lungs healthy.

It is possible to respire (release energy) without oxygen. This sometimes happens when people are doing hard exercise such as sprinting. When glucose is broken down without oxygen it is called **anaerobic** respiration. There are two main problems with anaerobic respiration. Firstly, it releases less than half the energy of that released by aerobic respiration. Secondly, it produces a substance called lactic acid that builds up in muscles and causes pain.

Anaerobic respiration

This flow chart follows the steps that happen during anaerobic respiration.

A runner goes into a very fast sprint near the end of a race.

The runner breathes hard, gasping for breath.

At the finish line, the runner breathes heavily for several minutes as their body takes in enough oxygen to return to normal aerobic respiration.

The heart and lungs cannot keep up with the extra demand for oxygen from their hard-working muscles.

To get extra energy, the muscle cells burn glucose using anaerobic respiration.

This gives the muscles the extra energy they need, but also produces waste lactic acid.

The lactic acid and the lack of oxygen make the runner's muscles ache. The runner feels exhausted and out of breath.

Flowchart Smart

Healthy lungs

Your lungs are yours for life so it makes sense to do what you can to protect them from harm. A cold or other respiratory infection can sometimes become very serious. There are ways to protect yourself.

Hands spread around 80 per cent of colds and flu. Washing your hands carefully and frequently using soap and water should reduce the risk of catching common infectious respiratory diseases. Cleaning your teeth can protect you from the germs in your mouth leading to infections. Brush your teeth at least twice a day and see your dentist at least every six months. If a cough or cold goes on too long or you get other lung problems such as shortness of breath, see a doctor as soon as possible.

We need lungs for speaking and singing. Vocal cords in the throat work a little like the way that air escaping from a balloon makes a noise. Squeezing and pulling the neck of the balloon changes the sound.

Get smart!

Your body needs water. You lose several cups of water each day through breathing alone. You replace that liquid by drinking. It is recommended that you drink 6–8 glasses of water a day. Water also helps keep your airways healthy and your lungs clean by helping to wash out old mucus lining the throat.

Our lungs and respiratory system are truly amazing. They help us get the oxygen we need to release energy from food. They remove wastes that could do us harm if they built up inside our body. The lungs even help us speak and sing. Air moving in and out of our lungs passes through a pair of vocal cords in the throat. The vocal cords change shape to make different sounds. Without lungs we would not even have a voice.

Glossary

aerobic type of respiration that uses oxygen

allergens substances that cause allergic reactions such as coughing or a swollen throat

alveoli tiny pouches or sacs of air at the end of the bronchioles in the lungs

anaerobic type of respiration that takes place without oxygen

bacteria microscopic living things, some of which can cause disease

blood vessel tube that carries blood around the body

bronchi pair of large tubes through which air passes between the trachea and the lungs

bronchioles tiny tubes that lead from the bronchi to the alveoli in the lungs

capillaries tiny blood vessels that connect the arteries and veins

carbon dioxide gas in the air

cells very small parts that together form all living things

chemical reaction chemical change that occurs when two or more substances combine to form a new substance

cilia tiny hair-like parts

circulatory system heart and blood vessels that move blood around the body

diaphragm large muscle between the chest and abdomen

diffusion when a substance moves from a region where it is in high concentration to a region where it is in low concentration

energy capacity to do work

fever unusually high body temperature caused by an infection

filter remove an unwanted substance

haemoglobin protein that transports oxygen in the blood

infection disease caused by bacteria that enter the body

inflame become swollen, red and painful

mitochondria parts in cells that use oxygen to release energy from food

nerve fibre that carries messages between the brain and the rest of the body

organs body parts such as the heart or liver

oxygen gas in the air

pressure pushing force

respiration process by which the body takes in oxygen and uses it to release energy from food

trachea tube that carries air in and out of the lungs

viruses tiny living things that can cause infection and disease

Find out more

Books

Exercise: From Birth to Old Age (Your Body for Life), Andrew Solway (Raintree, 2014)

Human Body: A Visual Encyclopedia, DK (DK Publishing, 2018)

Your Respiration and Circulation (Your Body by Numbers), Melanie Waldron (Raintree, 2014)

Websites

Discover more about the human body at:

www.bbc.co.uk/science/humanbody/body/index_interactivebody.shtml

Find out more about your lungs and breathing at:

www.dkfindout.com/uk/human-body/lungs-and-breathing/

Index